WELL DOC ANALY

THE TRUTH ABOUT THE

MALAYSIA'S MISSING

AIRPLANE MH370[PART 1]

PETER CHEW

PCET VENTURES (003368687-P)

Email:peterchew999@hotmail.my

© Peter Chew 2023

Cover Design : Peter Chew

Cover Image: Freepik Premium

Author: Peter Chew

Peter Chew is Global Issue Analyst, Mathematician, Inventor , Biochemist., Reviewer for Europe Publisher, Engineering Mathematics Lecturer and President of Research and Development Secondary School (IND) for Kedah State Association [2015-18]. Peter Chew received the 2019 Outstanding Analyst Award from IMRF (International Multidisciplinary Research Foundation). Analytical articles published in local and international media

Peter Chew also is CEO PCET, Ventures, Malaysia, PCET is a long research associate of IMRF , Institute of higher Education & Research with its HQ at India and Academic Chapters all over the world, PCET also Conference Partner in CoSMEd2021 by SEAMEO RECSAM.

Peter Chew as Keynote Speaker of the 8th International Conference on Computer Engineering and Mathematical Sciences (ICCEMS 2019) and the International Conference on Applications of Physics , Chemistry & Engineering Sciences, ICPCE 2020 . 2nd Plenary Speaker the 6th International Multidisciplinary Research Conference with a Mindanao Zonal Assembly on January 14, 2023, at the Immaculate Conception University, Bajada Campus, Davao City.

Special Talk Speaker at the 2019 International Conference on Advances in Mathematics, Statistics and Computer Science, the 100th CONF of the IMRF,2019, Goa , India.

Invite Speaker of the 24th Asian Mathematical Technology Conference (ATCM 2019) Leshan China and the 5^{th}(2020), 6th (2021) and 7th (2022) International Conference on Management, Engineering, Science, Social Sciences and Humanities by Society For Research Development(SRD).

Peter Chew is also Program Chair for the 11th International Conference on Engineering Mathematics and Physics (ICEMP 2022, Saint-Étienne, France | July 7-9, 2022) and Program Chair for the 12th International Conference on Engineering Mathematics and Physics (ICEMP 2023, Kuala Lumpur, Malaysia | July 5-7, 2023). For more information, please get it from this link Orcid: https://orcid.org/0000-0002-5935-3041.

WELL DOCUMENTED ANALYTICS. THE TRUTH ABOUT
THE MALAYSIA'S MISSING AIRPLANE MH370 [PART I]

TABLE OF CONTENTS

WELL DOCUMENTED ANALYTICS, THE TRUTH ABOUT
THE MALAYSIA'S MISSING AIRPLANE MH370 [PART 1]

TABLE OF CONTENTS

Well Documented Analytics. The truth about the Malaysia's Missing Airplane MH370(Part 1)

Families of Chinese passengers accuse Malaysia as 'murderer'[1]. Malaysia is accused of covering up MH370 issue. But Minister of Defense and Acting Minister of Transport Malaysia Datuk Seri Hishammuddin Tun Hussein- Malaysia is Not Hiding Information About The Loss Of Flight MH370.

The main misunderstanding Families of Chinese passengers is why did Malaysia confirm that MH 370 turned towards western Malaysia [Reuters : Malaysia military source says missing jet veered to west , March 11, 2014], and Malaysia decided to expand the search instead of only searching in the west? Therefore, the Families of Chinese passengers will think that Malaysia may be trying to hide some information.

The real reason is Reuters citing a incorrect information Malaysian Malay media(Berita Harian). Malaysia`s Berita Harian newspaper quoted Air force chief Rodzali Daud says missing jet veered to west

Reuters (Chinese) quoted the wrong information from Berita Harian newspaper , Malaysia Air force **chief** Rodzali Daud was last seen by military radar at 2:40 a.m. on Saturday, near Perak Island, at the northern end of the Strait of Malacca, Malaysia's Berita Harian newspaper reported earlier Tuesday, citing air force officer Rodzali Daud. The flight altitude is about 9,000 meters.

Reuters wrong information news above [March 11,2014] has been quote by some chinse famous media such as CCTV, World Wide Web, China Court International Website , China Daily and causing **greater misunderstanding**.

Chinese media [Zhong Shan] also quote Reuters wrong title 2014.03.11[Malaysia military source says missing jet veered to west] and, air force chief also later denied the news . Chinese media [Zhongshan] questioned the Malaysian government, what is the Malaysian government doing? Why provide conflicting information? This caused more misunderstandings.

On March 11, 2014, Malaysia decided to expand the search area to also search the eastern region. This is correct, because MH370 only has the possibility of turning back, which cannot be confirmed. Additionally, China claims to have found debris, possibly belonging to MH370 at East West coast of Malaysia on 9 march, 2014.

This book presents evidence that Malaysia is accused of covering up MH370 issue was wrong. Part 2 will analyse the theories of the disappearance of Malaysia Airlines Flight 370. A summary of the truth about the missing Malaysian plane MH 370 has been published in Malaysian media (national news). 13-4-2014.

On January 21, 2023, British Aerospace engineer Richard Godfrey, who is leading the tracking for MH370 has held a very successful meeting to discuss the progress of the WSPR technology which has pinpointed the most likely crash site for MH370 .

Peter Chew
Global Issue Analyst, Reviewer, Mathematician , Inventor and Biochemist.

Chapter 1: Malaysia Airlines Flight 370 .[1]   (Wikipedia)

1.1   Introduction   :Malaysia   Airlines   Flight 370: (MH370/MAS370)[2] was an international passenger flight operated by Malaysia Airlines that disappeared on 8 March 2014 while   flying   from Kuala   Lumpur   International Airport in Malaysia to its planned destination, Beijing Capital International   Airport .[3]   The   crew   of   the Boeing 777-200ER registered   as   9M-MRO,   last   communicated   with air traffic control (ATC) around 38 minutes after take off when the flight was over the South China Sea.

The aircraft was lost from ATC radar screens minutes later, but was tracked by military radar for another hour, deviating westward from its planned flight path, crossing the Malay Peninsula and Andaman Sea. It left radar range 200 nautical miles (370 km; 230 mi) northwest of Penang Island in north western Peninsular Malaysia.

With all 227 passengers and 12 crew aboard presumed dead, the disappearance of Flight 370 was the deadliest incident involving a Boeing 777 and the deadliest in Malaysia Airlines' history until it was surpassed in both regards by Malaysia Airlines Flight 17, which was shot down while flying over conflict-stricken eastern Ukraine four months later on 17 July 2014. The combined loss caused significant financial problems for Malaysia Airlines, which was renationalised by the Malaysian government in August 2014.

The search for the missing airplane became the most expensive in the history of aviation. It focused initially on the South China Sea and Andaman Sea, before analysis of the aircraft's automated communications with an Inmarsat satellite indicated a possible crash site somewhere in the southern Indian Ocean.

The lack of official information in the days immediately after the disappearance prompted fierce criticism from the Chinese public, particularly from relatives of the passengers, as most people on board Flight 370 were of Chinese origin.

Several pieces of debris washed ashore in the western Indian Ocean during 2015 and 2016; many of these were confirmed to have originated from Flight 370

1.2 Flight and disappearance

Flight 370 was a scheduled flight in the early morning of Saturday, 8 March 2014, from Kuala Lumpur, Malaysia, to Beijing, China. It was one of two daily flights operated by Malaysia Airlines from its hub at Kuala Lumpur International Airport (KLIA) to Beijing Capital International Airport— scheduled to depart at 00:35 local time (MYT; UTC+08:00) and arrive at 06:30 local time (CST; UTC+08:00).[4,5] On board were two pilots, 10 cabin crew, 227 passengers, and 14,296 kg (31,517 lb) of cargo. [3,6,7,8]

The planned flight duration was 5 hours and 34 minutes, which would consume an estimated 37,200 kg (82,000 lb) of jet fuel. The aircraft carried 49,100 kilograms (108,200 lb) of fuel, including reserves, allowing an endurance of 7 hours and 31 minutes.

The extra fuel was enough to divert to alternate airports—Jinan Yaoqiang International Airport and Hangzhou Xiaoshan International Airport—which would require 4,800 kg (10,600 lb) or 10,700 kg (23,600 lb), respectively, to reach from Beijing.[3,6,8]

1.3 Departure

At 00:42 MYT, Flight 370 took off from runway 32R,[3] and was cleared by air traffic control (ATC) to climb to flight level 180[9]—approximately 18,000 feet (5,500 m)—on a direct path to navigational waypoint IGARI (located at 6°56′12″N 103°35′6″E).

Voice analysis has determined that the first officer communicated with ATC while the flight was on the ground and that the Captain communicated with ATC after departure. [10]

Shortly after departure, the flight was transferred from the airport's ATC to "Lumpur Radar" air traffic control on frequency 132.6 MHz.

ATC over peninsular Malaysia and adjacent waters is provided by the Kuala Lumpur Area Control Centre (ACC); Lumpur Radar is the name of the frequency used for *en route* air traffic.[11]

At 00:46, Lumpur Radar cleared Flight 370 to flight level 350—approximately 35,000 ft (10,700 m). At 01:01, Flight 370's crew reported to Lumpur Radar that they had reached flight level 350, which they confirmed again at 01:08.[12]

1.4 Communication lost

The aircraft's final transmission was an automated position report, sent using the Aircraft Communications Addressing and Reporting System (ACARS) protocol at 01:06 MYT. [13,14,15]

Among the data provided in this message was the total fuel remaining: 43,800 kg (96,600 lb).[16] The last verbal signal to air traffic control occurred at 01:19:30, when Captain Zaharie acknowledged a transition from Lumpur Radar to Ho Chi Minh ACC:[17]

Lumpur Radar: "Malaysian three seven zero, contact Ho Chi Minh one two zero decimal nine. Good night."Flight 370: "Good night. Malaysian three seven zero."The crew was expected to signal ATC in Ho Chi Minh City as the aircraft passed into Vietnamese airspace, just north of the point where contact was lost.[18,19].The captain of another aircraft attempted to contact the crew of Flight 370 shortly after 01:30, using the international air distress frequency, to relay Vietnamese air traffic control's request for the crew to contact them; the captain said he was able to establish communication, but only heard "mumbling" and static.[20] Calls made to Flight 370's cockpit at 02:39 and 07:13 were unanswered, but acknowledged by the aircraft's satellite data unit.[21]

1.5 Southern Indian Ocean

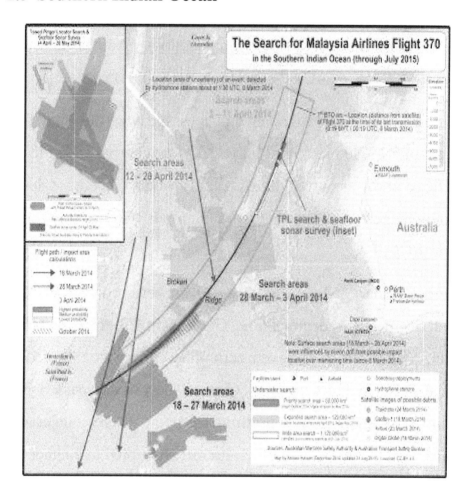

The emphasis of the search was shifted to the southern Indian Ocean west of Australia and within Australia's aeronautical and maritime Search and Rescue regions that extend to 75°E longitude.[22,23] . Accordingly, on 17 March, Australia agreed to manage the search in the southern locus from Sumatra to the southern Indian Ocean.[24,25]

1.6 Reference

1. **Wikipedia,** Malaysia Airlines Flight 370. https://en.wikipedia.org/wiki/Malaysia_Airlines_Flight_370

2. MH is the IATA designator and MAS is the ICAO airline designator. The flight was also marketed as China Southern Airlines Flight 748 (CZ748/CSN748) through a codeshare agreement.[4]

3. *MacLeod, Calum; Winter, Michael; Gray, Allison (8 March 2014). "Beijing-bound flight from Malaysia missing". USA Today. Archived from the original on 11 November 2020. Retrieved 3 May 2014.*

4. *"Tweet". Twitter. Flightradar24. 7 March 2014. Retrieved 24 October 2014.*

5. *Jump up to:[a,b]* *"Malaysia Airlines 2Q loss widens. Restructuring is imminent but outlook remains bleak"*. CAPA Centre For Aviation. 28 August 2014. *Retrieved 24 October 2014*. The only significant cut MAS implemented in 2Q2014 was on the Beijing route, which is now served with one daily flight. (MH370 was one of two daily flights MAS had operated to Beijing.)

6. Factual Information, Safety Investigation: Malaysia Airlines MH370 Boeing 777-200ER (9M-MRO)" (PDF). *Malaysia: Malaysia Ministry of Transport. 8 March 2014. Archived from* Information.pdf the original (PDF) *on 9 March 2015*. Retrieved 9 March 2015. {{cite web}}: Check |url= value (help)

7. Shah, Aliza (18 January 2018). "Norwegian vessel to arrive at MH370 search area this weekend". New Straits Times. Kuala Lumpur. Archived from the original on 7 February 2018. Retrieved 19 January 2018.

8. ASN Aircraft accident Boeing 777-212ER 9V-SQK Singapore-Changi International Airport (SIN)". *aviation-safety.net*. Retrieved 30 May 2020.

9. Aircraft altitude is given as feet above sea level and measured, at higher altitudes, by air pressure, which declines as altitude above sea level increases. Using a standard sea level pressure and formula, the nominal altitude of a given air pressure can be determined—referred to as the "pressure altitude". A flight level is the pressure altitude in hundreds of feet. For example, flight level 350 corresponds to an altitude where air pressure is 179 mmHg (23.9 kPa), which is nominally 35,000 ft (10,700 m) but does not indicate the true altitude.

10. Ship hired to find MH370 arrives in search zone". *The Star*. Sydney. Reuters. 23 January 2018. Archived from the original on 12 June 2018. Retrieved 23 January 2018.

11. Airspace Delegated to Malaysia" (PDF). *Department of Civil Aviation Malaysia*. Department of Civil Aviation Malaysia. 25 August 2011. Retrieved 24 October 2014.

12. Documents: Preliminary report on missing Malaysia Airlines Flight 370". Malaysia Department of Civil Aviation. Retrieved 22 October 2014 – via CNN.

13. "MH 370 – Definition of Underwater Search Areas" (PDF). Australian Transport Safety Bureau. 26 June 2014. Archived (PDF) from the original on 27 August 2014. Retrieved 12 April 2015. "The Search for MH370: Reports". Australian Transport Safety Bureau.

14. "MH370 PC live updates / 530 17th March". Out of Control Videos. Archived from the original on 17 March 2014. Retrieved 16 July 2014. Timing of ACARS deactivation unclear. Last ACARS message at 01:07 was not necessarily point at which system was turned off

15.Jump up to : "Signalling Unit Log for (9M-MRO) Flight MH370" (PDF). Inmarsat/Malaysia Department of Civil Aviation. Archived from the original (PDF) on 4 March 2016. Retrieved 29 June 2014.

16. <u>MH370 – Flight Path Analysis Update</u>" (PDF). *Australian Transport Safety Bureau*. <u>Australian Transport Safety Bureau</u>. 8 October 2014. Retrieved 15 November 2014.

*17.*Factual Information, Safety Investigation: Malaysia Airlines MH370 Boeing 777-200ER (9M-MRO)" (PDF). *Malaysia: Malaysia Ministry of Transport. 8 March 2014. Archived from* Information.pdf the original (PDF) *on 9 March 2015.* Retrieved 9 March 2015. {{cite web}}: Check |url= value (help)

18. <u>FlightRadar24.com MH370 7 March 2014</u>". Retrieved 12 February 2019.

19. "<u>Malaysian Airlines System (MH) No. 370 ✈ 08-Mar-2014 WMKK / KUL – ZBAA / PEK</u>. FlightAware. <u>Archived</u> *from the original on 8 March 2014.*

20. "<u>Pilot: I established contact with plane</u>". *New Straits Times*. <u>AsiaOne</u>. 9 March 2014.

21. Simon Denyer, Robert Barnes & Chico Harlan (9 March 2014). "Debris spotted may be from missing Malaysian Airline flight". *The Washington Post*. Archived from the original on 9 March 2014.

22. *Arrangements in Australia". Australian Maritime Safety Authority. Archived from the original on 24 February 2015. Retrieved 12 November 2014.*

23 *"National Search and Rescue Manual – June 2014 edition" (PDF). Australia Maritime Safety Authority. p. 231. Archived from the original (PDF) on 12 April 2015. Retrieved 12 November 2014.*

24. Australia agrees to lead search in Indian Ocean for missing Malaysia Airlines flight MH370". The Canberra Times. 17 March 2014. Archived from the original on 17 May 2014. Retrieved 12 April 2015.

25."Missing MH370: Australia to lead southern search for MH370". The Star. 17 March 2014.

Chapter 2: Families of Chinese passengers MH 370

2.1 Families of Chinese passengers accuse Malaysia as 'murderer'[1]. Malaysia is accused of covering up MH370 issue. March 25, 2014.

A representative reads complaints about the Malaysian government made by relatives of Chinese passengers aboard Malaysia Airlines MH370 at the Lido hotel in Beijing.

The loved ones of the Chinese passengers on missing Malaysia Airlines flight 370 have lashed out in at Malaysia after being informed by the country's prime minister the plane and its 239 passengers were believed lost.

A joint statement issued on Tuesday, the family and friends wrote, ""Malaysian Prime Minister Najib Razak, without any direct evidence, announced the plane crashed in the southern Indian Ocean and none of the passengers survived.

Since the Malaysian government announced loss of contact with the plane on March 8, Malaysia Airlines, the Malaysian government and the Malaysian military made every effort to postpone and conceal the truth in the past 18 days, attempting to deceive passengers' families as well as the world."

The statement follows Malaysian Prime Minister Najib Razak's announcement on Monday night that flight MH370 ended in the southern Indian Ocean.

The friends and families, however, were only angered by the announcement. According to a China Daily reporter on hand at the Metropark Lido Hotel in Beijing, where the group has been staying, some of the loved ones went to the Malaysian Embassy in Beijing to ask for details.

"Last night after hearing Malaysian Prime Minister's announcement, all the relatives of MH370 passengers responded in anguish. Some of them smashed the chairs and clashed with the police in the Metropark Lido Hotel. To avoid this situation, all the chairs have been linked up with each other by ropes," The China Daily reporter said. The frustration of a 17-day search with few details appeared to have boiled over for the group of supporters.

The joint statement continued:

"These mean and shameless acts not only tortured families of passengers, but also misled and delayed search and rescue operations. It caused wasted efforts and loss of rescue opportunities.

If our relatives - the 154 Chinese passengers onboard - lost their lives, then Malaysia Airlines, the Malaysian government and the Malaysian military are the real murderer.

We make the strongest protest and condemnation and will call to account their guilt by any possible means."

2.2 Chinese relatives demand apology from Malaysia.

March 30, 2014[2].

Newly arrived Chinese relatives of passengers on board the missing Malaysia Airlines flight MH370 hold a sign as they speak to reporters at a hotel in Subang Jaya, Malaysia, Sunday March 30, 2014.

KUALA LUMPUR, Malaysia — Several dozen Chinese relatives of passengers on Flight 370 demanded Sunday that Malaysia apologize for its handling of the search for the missing plane and for the prime minister's statement saying it crashed into the southern Indian Ocean.

Holding up banners that read **"We want evidence, truth, dignity"** in Chinese, and "Hand us the murderer. Tell us the truth. Give us our relatives back" in English, the group staged a protest at a hotel near Kuala Lumpur just hours after flying in from Beijing.

Two-thirds of the 227 passengers aboard the Malaysia Airlines plane that disappeared March 8 en route to Beijing from Kuala Lumpur were Chinese, and the plane's disappearance has sparked broad outrage in China, with celebrities joining in and travel agencies announcing boycotts.

Flight booking website eLong said it was suspending Malaysia Airlines flight sales until the relatives are satisfied with the government's response. Last Wednesday, Chinese touring agency CYTS said it would stop offering tours to Malaysia because of safety concerns.

Even popular actress Zhang Ziyi spoke out. "Malaysian government, you have hurt the entire world. … You have misjudged the persistence in seeking truth by the world's people, including all the Chinese," she wrote on her microblog.

The protesters Sunday repeatedly chanted slogans in Chinese: **"We want evidence! We want the truth! We want our relatives!". The video link is https://youtu.be/COR4iKx0CZo**

Jiang Hui, the relatives' designated representative, said they wanted a government apology for what they see as missteps in the initial handling of the disaster as well as Prime Minister Najib Razak's statement that indicated the plane had crashed with no survivors. Jiang said the relatives felt the conclusion was announced without sufficient evidence.

"We also request that Malaysia Airlines and the Malaysian government apologize for making the conclusion on March 24, without direct evidence or a sense of responsibility, that the plane was destroyed and people died," Jiang said.

He said the group wanted to meet with airline and government officials, although he stopped short of saying that included Najib, as earlier proposed by some relatives.

In Beijing, tensions are still high at a hotel where Chinese relatives have been meeting with Malaysian representatives. On Sunday, one woman asking questions called Malaysia Airlines "criminal suspects" to applause among the crowd of about 250 relatives.

Relatives asked why materials being shown to them, including PowerPoint presentations, were in English and not Chinese. Najib went on television on March 24 to say that based on radar and satellite analysis, the Boeing 777 had crashed somewhere in the southern Indian Ocean, but there were lingering questions because there was no physical evidence.

That wariness on the part of the relatives was also fueled by missteps at the beginning of the search, which started in waters off Vietnam, then swung to areas west of Malaysia and Indonesia, and then as radar and satellite information was further analyzed, to southwest of Australia and now to a second zone farther northeast.

"We hope that in these days, we can meet with technical teams involved in the search, and hold talks with Malaysia Airlines and the Malaysian government. We hope that these discussions will not be like they had been in Beijing, with wishy-washy answers," Jiang said.

2.3 Relatives of passengers demand Malaysia 'tell the truth'[3].

March 19, 2014. https://www.washingtonpost.com/world/malaysian-authorities-cede-search-control/2014/03/18/3d112454-ae91-11e3-96dc-d6ea14c099f9_story.html

The search for Malaysia Airlines Flight 370 has two points of focus: finding physical wreckage and determining an explanation of the suspected "deliberate act" that led to the plane's disappearance.

KUALA LUMPUR, Malaysia — Shouting and wailing in anger and grief, a handful of Chinese relatives of passengers on a missing airliner burst into the media auditorium in the Malaysian capital on Wednesday, and unfurled a banner demanding the government "tell the truth."

2.4 Reference

1. Families of Chinese passengers accuse Malaysia as 'murderer' China Daily Updated: 2014-03-25

https://www.chinadaily.com.cn/world/2014planemissing/2014-03-25/content_17376415.htm

2. Chinese relatives demand apology from Malaysia. Associated Press. https://nypost.com/2014/03/30/chinese-relatives-demand-apology-from-malaysia/

3. Chico Harlan, Simon Denyer ,Ashley Halsey III . Relatives of passengers demand Malaysia 'tell the truth'[3] March 19, 2014. https://www.washingtonpost.com/world/malaysian-authorities-cede-search-control/2014/03/18/3d112454-ae91-11e3-96dc-d6ea14c099f9_story.html

Chapter 3: Minister of Defense :- Malaysia Is Not Hiding Information About The Loss Of Flight MH370.

3.1 MH370 crash: Singapore defends Malaysia's efforts on missing plane[1]. 28 Mar 2014

Singapore came to Malaysia's defence after scathing criticism of Kuala Lumpur's handling of the disappearance of a passenger plane with 239 people on board. Singapore Foreign Minister K. Shanmugam also said Malaysia's Southeast Asian neighbours did what they could to help in the early days of searching for Malaysia Airlines flight MH370, but most of them lack the necessary resources for large scale assistance.

"I think some of the criticisms are unfair," Shanmugam told the Foreign Correspondents Association in Singapore on Friday."I don't think enough account has been taken of the fact that there was very little to go on, very little that the Malaysians or anyone knew about the matter," he said, describing the plane's disappearance as a "most unusual, bizarre situation". Flight MH370, carrying mostly Chinese nationals, vanished from civilian radar on March 8 while on a flight from Kuala Lumpur to Beijing.

A massive international search is currently focused on the southern Indian Ocean, where the aircraft is thought to have crashed after mysteriously veering off course. Malaysia has come under criticism for alleged incompetence and been accused of a cover-up, especially by families of the Chinese passengers, as well as from China's media.

"In the early days of their daily press briefings after the plane went missing, Malaysian officials made a series of contradictory statements that added to the confusion".

Notably, there have been about-turns regarding the crucial sequence of events in the plane's cockpit before it veered off course, and Malaysia's armed forces have been criticised for failing to intercept the diverted plane when it appeared on military radar.

Shanmugam said Malaysia's Southeast Asian neighbours responded well to the situation, but lacked the assets that the United States, China and other countries had. "I think there was certainly no lack of will in terms of wanting to cooperate," he said. "But in order to do something like this we also need the assets and the resources."

3.2 MH370: China will always stand by Malaysia in dealing with incident, says ambassador[2]. 22 May 2014

China has vowed that Malaysia will not face the current unprecedented disappearance of a Malaysia Airlines (MAS) aircraft alone.

Its ambassador to Malaysia, Huang Hui kang, said China was committed to help and **trust Malaysia's efforts in handling the situation**, which he described as a consistent commitment from the beginning.

"Our relations have never been affected by any unexpected single incident. Through the cooperation in dealing with the incident, our relations have become stronger and closer. "These (have) once again proved a friend in need, is a friend indeed," he said at a press briefing in conjunction with the 40th anniversary of diplomatic relations between China and Malaysia here Thursday.

On March 8, MAS flight MH370 disappeared with 227 passengers and 12 crewmembers on board the Boeing 777-200ER aircraft. Almost two-thirds of the passengers are Chinese nationals.

"If you look at the progress that has been made in dealing with the incident from the very beginning, the Chinese government and its people firmly stand side by side with Malaysia," said Huang. He added that China had organised a large-scale international search and rescue operation, and also mobilised its satellites, ships and aircraft.

He said China had put so much effort in dealing with the incident as two-thirds of the passengers were its citizens. "It is the Chinese government's responsibility - no matter how much money we have spent - we are doing our best to assist Malaysia," he said.

3.3 Family criticizes deceitful Malaysian Defense Minister: No concealment. 19-3-2014

Malaysia Airlines has lost contact and has not yet been found. The family members turned from anxiety to anger, criticizing Malaysia for cheating, talking nonsense, and delaying the progress of the search and rescue.

The Minister of Defense of Malaysia emphasized in an exclusive interview that the information is open and transparent, and they absolutely did not Deliberately concealing the truth as criticized by the outside world.

Malaysian Defense Minister Hishammuddin: "Absolutely no human life is at stake, how can we hide it." Hishammuddin also emphasized that information is absolutely transparent and that human lives are at stake. They have put national security in second place.

Malaysian Defense Minister Hishammuddin: **"We strive for transparency because we share military information."**

In addition, when asked how to explain to the family members, Hishammuddin expressed emotionally that he sincerely prayed for them, and it was said that he could not control his emotions at one point and choked up his face

Family members of Chinese passengers: "Malaysia is talking nonsense and not telling the truth. He is a deceit." The family members in Beijing directly scolded them. No wonder they were so angry.

It has been more than 10 days since the flight lost contact. Previously, the Malaysian authorities were confused and could not give an explanation. Although the Prime Minister came forward to announce the latest news, the family members still did not buy it. Family members of the Chinese passengers:

"Originally, you changed the west side to the east side. If you could track satellite signals for search and rescue, wouldn't it be effective now?"

Note: The main misunderstanding is why did Malaysia confirm that MH 370 turned towards western Malaysia, and Malaysia decided to expand the search instead of only searching in the west? Therefore, the family members of the Chinese passengers will think that Malaysia may be trying to hide some information .

3.4 Reference

1. MH370 crash: Singapore defends Malaysia's efforts on missing plane[2] The Star . NATION . 28 Mar 2014

https://www.thestar.com.my/news/nation/2014/03/28/mh370-singapore-fm-defends-malaysia/

2. MH370: China will always stand by Malaysia in dealing with incident, says ambassador[2]. The Star . NATION 22-5-14.

https://www.thestar.com.my/news/nation/2014/05/22/mh370-china-will-stand-by-msia

3. FTV . **Family criticizes deceitful Malaysian Defense Minister: No concealment. 18-3-2014**

https://movies.yahoo.com.tw/%E5%AE%B6%E5%B1%AC%E6%89%B9%E6%AC%BA%E9%A8%99-%E9%A6%AC%E5%9C%8B%E5%9C%8B%E9%98%B2%E9%83%A8%E9%95%B7-%E6%B2%92%E9%9A%B1%E7%9E%9E-100109208.html

Chapter 4: The real reason that Malaysia is accused of Hiding Information About The Loss Of Flight MH370

Some media titles and information such as Malaysia's Berita Harian newspaper **are incorrect, causing misunderstanding** .

4.1 The title of the video by Malaysia Media, astro AWANI are wrong. **Title video : The TUDM confirmed that the MH370 turned around . [TUDM sahkan MH 370 berpatah balik]** .[1]

TUDM sahkan MH370 berpatah balik

If listen to video , Air force chief Rodzali Daud is saying there is possibility MH370 turn back, he is not confirmed that the MH370 turned back . The title of the video is missing an important word "possibility"

Due to the possibility of MH370 turning back, the search area has also been expanded to the west, not just the search to the east.

But since there is only the possibility of turning back, Malaysia still has to search the Eastern District. If the return of MH370 is confirmed, there is no need to search the Eastern District.

from the news Malaysia Airlines:

4.2 Object found by Vietnam navy thought to be part of missing plane.[2] 9 Mar 2014

• Debris thought to be from the missing Malaysian Airlines flight has been found in waters 80 km southwest off Vietnam's Tho Chu island. Officials are waiting for daylight to examine the discovery by a Vietnamese navy plane, with the debris yet to be confirmed as connected to flight MH370. Lack of concentrated debris means plane may have disintegrated at 35,000 ft, investigators say.

4.3 On 9 march, 2014. China claims to have found debris, possibly belonging to MH370.[3]

In addition, on 9 march, 2014. China claims to have found debris, possibly belonging to MH370 at East West coast of Malaysia.

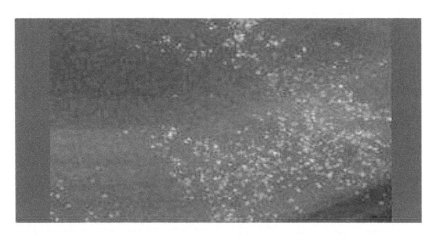

China dakwa jumpa
serpihan pesawat,
mungkin milik MH370

Astro Awani
Mac 9, 2014 14:25 MYT

Gambar serpihan oleh penumpang China yang
dimuatnaik laman Weibo

A photo of the wreckage by a Chinese passenger uploaded to Weibo

Some plane debris has been reported to be found off the East-West coast of Malaysia, but it has yet to be confirmed as belonging to the missing Malaysia Airlines flight MH370.

Senior official of the Civil Aviation Administration of China, Li Jiaxiang, said that the debris was found in the area of longitude 103.29 degrees east and latitude 6.42 degrees north.

"However, this discovery is still awaiting confirmation from the search team that arrived at the location," he said in a news report.

"We are still not sure of the exact location of the plane, and are still hoping for a miracle that all the passengers are safe," Li said as reported by China News. "It is also not clear at this point if the plane was involved in a terrorist attack," he added.

China claims to have found debris, possibly belonging to MH370 at East West coast of Malaysia (Video) .[4]

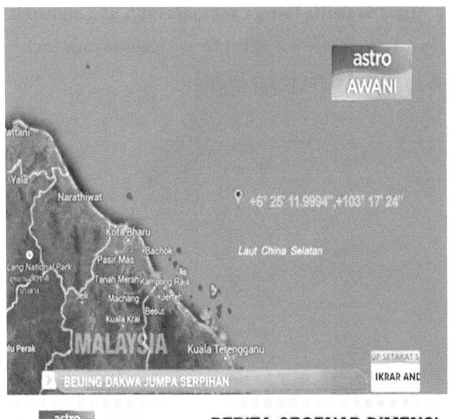

So Malaysia is right to decide to expand the search area instead of only looking west, as MH370 only has the possibility of turning back [meaning it is still possible to be in the eastern District], China claims to have found debris, possibly belonging to MH370 at East West coast of Malaysia on 9 March 2014.

4.4 Malaysia Berita Harian newspaper title and content is wrong. Title :_There is a signal for the plane to turn back.[5]

Ada isyarat pesawat berpatah balik

2014/03/10 - 05:53:23 AM

 ✉ Emel Kawan 🖨 Cetak

Like 10 Tweet 1   +1 0

"

Radar tentera ada mengesan pergerakan pesawat berpatah balik dan menyebabkan operasi mencari dan menyelamat diperluaskan ke sekitar perairan Pulau Pinang"

Rodzali Daud,
Panglima TUDM

> Kuala Lumpur: Kehilangan pesawat MH370 terus diselubungi misteri apabila ada isyarat pada radar menunjukkan ia berpatah balik menghala Kota Bharu pada jam 2.40 pagi hari kejadian kelmarin.

Menurut sumber, ia dikesan menara kawalan Pangkalan Tentera Udara Diraja Malaysia (TUDM), Butterworth serta bilik kawalan beberapa kapal Tentera Laut Diraja Malaysia (TLDM) yang mengawasi keselamatan kawasan Laut China Selatan serta Unit Kawalan dan Pengawasan Trafik Udara Singapura.

- 'ELAK ROSAK REPUTASI'
- Tragedi MH370: Harapan jumpa kotak hitam cerah
- Tragedi MH370: 'Saya lebih optimistik kali ini'
- Jambatan ketiga perkukuh persahabatan
- 3 produk pelangsing badan beracun

PILIHAN TERTINGGI

- Dahi bengkak kegilaan baharu di Jepun

PILIHAN EDITOR

- Lima kementerian dipanggil
- Bicara Kassim hina Islam 6, 7 Mei
- SMS, Facebook kesan anak, kereta dilarikan
- Tiga beranak curi motosikal ditahan

In addition, Malaysia Berita Harian newspaper also mention **the disappearance of flight MH370 continues to be shrouded in mystery when there is a signal on the radar showing that it turned back towards Kota Bharu at 2.40am on the day of the incident yesterday**.

Malaysia Media, myMetroTV report correctly.

Title : Flight MH370 may try to turn back.[6]

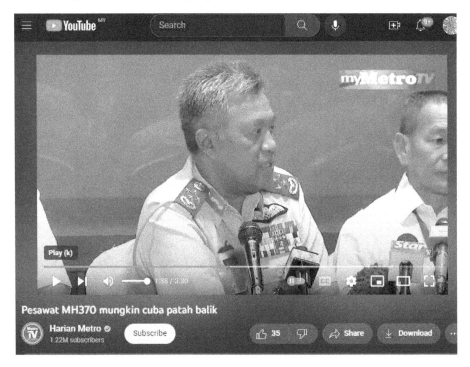

If listen to this video[1.26] , Air force chief Rodzali Daud is saying there is possibility MH370 turn back

4.5 Reuters[7] quoted the wrong information from Berita Harian newspaper , Malaysia, causing more misunderstandings.

Title Reuters: Malaysia military source says missing jet veered to west . By Niluksi Koswanage, Eveline Danubrata. MARCH 11, 2014

As mention, Malaysia Berita Harian newspaper mention **the disappearance of flight MH370 continues to be shrouded in mystery when there is a signal on the radar showing that it turned back towards Kota Bharu at 2.40am on the day of the incident yesterday**.

Reuters quoted the wrong information from Berita Harian newspaper , Malaysia causing more misunderstandings.

Malaysia's Berita Harian newspaper quoted Air Force chief Rodzali Daud as saying the plane was last detected at 2:40 a.m. by military radar near the island of Pulau Perak at the northern end of the Strait of Malacca. It was flying about 1,000 metres (3,280 feet) lower than its previous altitude, he was quoted as saying.

Malaysia's Berita Harian newspaper quoted Air Force chief Rodzali Daud as saying the plane was last detected at 2:40 a.m. by military radar near the island of Pulau Perak at the northern end of the Strait of Malacca.

It was flying about 1,000 metres (3,280 feet) lower than its previous altitude, he was quoted as saying.

Reuters (**Chinese**)[8]quoted the wrong information from Berita Harian newspaper , Malaysia Air force officer Rodzali Daud was last seen by military radar at 2:40 a.m. on Saturday, near Perak Island, at the northern end of the Strait of Malacca, Malaysia's

Berita Harian newspaper reported earlier Tuesday, citing air force officer Rodzali Daud. The flight altitude is about 9,000 meters.

Reuters wrong information news march 11,2014 has been quote by some chinse famous media such as CCTV a and causing more misunderstandings

4.6 Some Chinese media quoted, according to Reuters news on March 11, 2014, mentioned the Malay military: radar has tracked MH370 to the Strait of Malacca

i) China famous media._CCTV March 12, 2014 04: 15[9]

ii) China famous media._CCTV March 12, 2014 21: 21[10]

iii)World Wide Web .[11]

World Wide Web mention Reuters quoted Malaysian military sources on March 11 as saying that the Malaysian military believed that their radar had detected the missing Malaysia Airlines passenger plane flying over the Strait of Malacca.

A Malaysian military official said: "The plane changed its course after flying over Kota Bharu and entered low-altitude airspace, allowing the plane to enter the Strait of Malacca.

iv) China Court International Website .[12]

v) Reuters wrong information news march 11,2014 has been quote by China media, China Daily.[13]

4.7 Malaysia denies detecting missing plane in Strait of Malacca 12-3-2014.[14]

i) Report on Chinese media.

Malaysia's air force chief has denied that the country's military last detected missing Malaysia Airlines flight MH370 west of the Strait of Malacca.

Malaysian Air Force Commander Daoud said on Wednesday (March 12) that the authorities have not yet ruled out the possibility that the Malaysia Airlines passenger plane had changed its flight direction before it disappeared, but he denied that the missing passenger plane was far away from its original route when it was last detected. reports.

Daoud said in a statement that the air force had not yet ruled out the possibility that the missing airliner had diverted to return flight before disappearing from radar screens. He said the scope of the search and rescue operation has therefore been extended to adjacent waters, off the west coast of Malaysia. Daoud, however, denied the report by Malaysia's Daily News on Tuesday.

Air force chief denies

The report quoted Daoud as saying that the last time the missing flight appeared on the radar screen of the control tower was at 2:40 a.m. local time on Saturday (8th). The plane was approaching the Strait of Malacca in western Malaysia.

Commander Daoud said, "I would like to declare that I did not make relevant remarks," and Malaysia's "Daily News" published "obviously inaccurate and incorrect reports.

"Malaysia's military believes it has tracked the missing Malaysia Airlines jet by radar over the Strait of Malacca, a source in the Malaysian military told Reuters, far from where the plane last made contact with the Civil Aviation Authority.

"After flying over Kota Bharu, the aircraft changed course and entered the airspace over the Strait of Malacca," the official said.

The head of Malaysia's Civil Aviation Authority, Azharuddin Azharuddin, said the international search for the missing Malaysia Airlines plane had been extended to the Andaman Sea. North of Sumatra, Indonesia is the Andaman Sea.

ii) China TV. The Malaysian military denies that the passenger plane turned back to the Strait of Malacca. Mar 12, 2014 .[15] Commander Daoud said, "I would like to declare that I did not make relevant remarks,"

iii) Statement by TUDM Chief on Berita Harian report on Malaysia Airlines Flight MH370 March 12, 2014.[16]

Panglima Tentera Udara (Chief of the Royal Malaysian Air Force), General Tan Sri Dato'Sri Rodzali Daud, issued the following statement late last night (11 March 2014). The statement corrects a report in Malaysia's Berita Harian newspaper that ascribed remarks on the air turn back of Malaysia Airlines Flight MH370 towards the Malacca Strait to PTU. We reproduce PTU's statement in full.

OFFICIAL STATEMENT BY CHIEF OF ROYAL MALAYSIAN AIR FORCE ON

BERITA HARIAN NEWS ARTICLE DATED 11ᵗʰ MARCH 2014 ON SEARCH AND RESCUE OPERATIONS IN THE STRAITS OF MALACCA

1. I refer to the Berita Harian news article dated 11th March 2014 on Search and Rescue Operations in the Straits of Malacca which (in Bahasa Malaysia) referred to me as making the following statements:

The RMAF Chief confirmed that RMAF Butterworth airbase detected the location signal of the airliner as indicating that it turned back from its original heading to the direction of Kota Bahru, Kelantan, and was believed to have pass through the airspace of the East Coast of and Northern Peninsular Malaysia. The last time the plane was detected by the air control tower was in the vicinity of Pulau Perak in the Straits of Malacca at 2.40 in the morning before the signal disappeared without any trace, he said.

2. I wish to state that I did not make any such statements as above, what occurred was that the Berita Harian journalist asked me if such an incident occurred as detailed in their story, however I did not give any answer to the question, instead what I said to the journalist was **"Please refer to the statement which I have already made on 9 March 2014, during the press conference with the Chief of Defense Force at the Sama-Sama Hotel, Kuala Lumpur International Airport".**

3. What I stated during that press conference was,

The RMAF has not ruled out the possibility of an air turn back on a reciprocal heading before the aircraft vanished from the radar and this resulted in the Search and Rescue Operations being widen to the vicinity of the waters of Pulau Pinang.

4. I request this misreporting be amended and corrected to prevent further misinterpretations of what is clearly an inaccurate and incorrect report.

5. Ccurrently the RMAF is examining and analyzing all possibilities as regards to the airliner's flight paths subsequent to its disappearance. However for the time being, it would not be appropriate for the RMAF to issue any official conclusions as to the aircraft's flight path until a high amount of certainty and verification is achieved. However all ongoing search operations are at the moment being conducted to cover all possible areas where the aircraft could have gone down in order to ensure no possibility is overlooked.

6. In aaddition, I would like to state to the media that all information and developments will be released via official statements and press conferences as soon as possible and when appropriate. Our current efforts are focused upon on finding the aircraft as soon as possible.

Thank You

GENERAL TAN SRI DATO'SRI RODZALI BIN DAUD RMAF
Chief of Royal Malaysian Air Force

4.8 Some analysts are drawing conclusions based on erroneous media headlines and information.Zhong Shan said: Malaysia Airline, Malaysia Government, what are you doing .[17]

Reuters error message 2014.03.11[Malaysia military source says missing jet veered to west] was quoted by Chinese media, air force chief also later denied the news being used by the Chinese media to question the Malaysian government, what is the Malaysian government doing? Why provide conflicting information? . This caused more misunderstandings.

4.9 Conclusion

The real reason is Reuters citing a incorrect information Malaysian Malay media(Berita Harian). Malaysia`s Berita Harian newspaper quoted Air force chief Rodzali Daud says missing jet veered to west.

Reuters wrong information news above [March 11,2014] has been quote by some chinse famous media such as CCTV, World Wide Web, China Court International Website , China Daily and causing **greater misunderstanding**.

On March 11, 2014, Malaysia decided to expand the search area to also search the eastern region. This is correct, because MH370 only has the possibility of turning back, which cannot be confirmed.

Additionally, China claims to have found debris, possibly belonging to MH370 at East West coast of Malaysia on 9 march, 2014.

4.10. The latest MH 370 information.

MH370 TRACKING MEETING "A GREAT SUCCESS "[18]

By **Geoffrey Thomas** January 21, 2023

British Aerospace engineer Richard Godfrey, who is leading the tracking for MH370 has held a very successful meeting to discuss the progress of the WSPR technology which has pinpointed the most likely crash site for MH370. It is highly likely that this work will be the basis of the next search.

Mr Godfrey has published this map (under) of the MH370 location based on his WSPR technology and you can read the full report here and you can read his latest tracking meeting update below.

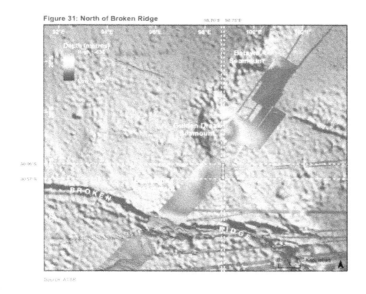

Figure 31: North of Broken Ridge

Mr Godfrey posted to his website the following detail.

"The meeting on WSPR technology was a great success. There were a significant number of participants from all over the globe and from various time zones. Some participants had 2 feet of new snow outside their window, others were sweltering at 34°C (93°F) and high humidity.

With multiple presenters (Prof. Simon Maskell, Dr Hannes Coetzee, Dominik Bugmann and myself), the Google Meet technology was stretched to the limit. Internet connections generally held up globally, with one short exception.

"Dr Robert Westphal and his collaborator Dr Karl Herrmann were not able to attend, but their early pioneer work and ongoing research are held in high honour, despite the strong opposing winds that caused them to retreat from public life. Rob is the father of the idea to use WSPR to track MH370.

"There is definitely a momentum building in using WSPR to detect and track aircraft and in using WSPR to help identify the crash location of MH370. I personally found the meeting very encouraging.

The meeting overran, as there was such great interest in our work evidenced by a large number of very good and perceptive questions being asked and answered. In hindsight, we should have recorded the meeting.

"Prof. Simon Maskell observed: "I thought it was particularly reassuring that the questions that we can't answer easily are precisely those that we are working towards generating compelling answers for."

It was also clear, that it is perfectly acceptable in scientific circles to say, that we don't know the full answer to that question yet, but we also have the same question and are working on the answer, and we will let you know our findings in due course.

"Dr. Hannes Coetzee outlined the major differences between classical radar and WSPR technology. A typical airport radar has a pulse width of 1 μs and the energy illuminating any object is small despite the transmission power of 1.1 MW and pulse rate between 300 and 1,200 pulses per second.

WSPR has a coherent integration time of 110.6 seconds and a transmission power of typically 1 W, resulting in a similar order of magnitude of energy illuminating the target aircraft. Hannes also pointed out the WSPR processing removes short and medium-term ionospheric fluctuations.

"Dominik Bugmann showed how WSPR signals from his radio shack in Switzerland can be received in Australia with the WSPR protocol confirming receipt of the signal and how the receiving station software determined the signal-to-noise ratio and frequency drift deviations.

He also demonstrated how the interim landing points of a multiple-hop ionospheric propagation aligned with the target aircraft position and the great circle paths of multiple intersecting anomalous WSPR links.

"The participants thanked us for the great work and the obvious thousands of hours invested in WSPR technology and using that to help solve the mystery of MH370.

It was once again evident to all participants that the combination of Inmarsat satellite data, Boeing aircraft performance data, 39 items of likely or confirmed MH370 floating debris, the UWA drift analysis data and our work using WSPR technology all point to the same crash location around 30°S to 32°S.

"It was equally clear that the MH370 crash location could be just outside of the previously searched areas in this latitude range. However, the absence of the IFE connection expected at around 00:21:06 UTC (approximately 90 seconds after 00:19:37 UTC) as well as the analysis of the BFO data by Ian Holland of the DSTG, which shows an accelerating rate of descent of between 14,800 fpm and 25,300 fpm at 00:19:37 UTC, may well both separately set a limit to the maximum possible distance of the crash location from the 7th Arc.

In summary, this information narrows the area for any future underwater search for MH370 and increases the probability of finding the main wreckage of MH370."

4.11 Reference

1. astro AWANI The TUDM confirmed that the MH370 turned around . [TUDM sahkan MH 370 berpatah balik]
https://youtu.be/pwxBVl1ezm8

2. Josh Halliday *and* Michael Safi . Malaysia Airlines: object found by Vietnam navy thought to be part of missing plane – live.   the Guardian   Sun   9   Mar   2014 18.28 .
https://www.theguardian.com/world/2014/mar/09/malaysia-airlines-missing-plane-investigation-widens-live

3. Astro Awani   China claims to have found debris, possibly belonging to MH370 . 9 march, 2014.
 https://www.astroawani.com/berita-malaysia/china-dakwa-jumpa-serpihan-pesawat-mungkin-milik-mh370-31538

4. Astro Awani (Video)   China claims to have found debris, possibly belonging to MH370.
https://www.astroawani.com/video-politik/beijing-dakwa-jumpa-serpihan-mh370-1655449

5. Malaysia Berita Harian. There is a signal for the plane to turn back. https://peraktoday.com.my/2014/03/ada-isyarat-pesawat-berpatah-balik/

6. myMetroTV Flight MH370 may try to turn back. Mar 9, 2014 . https://youtu.be/ZpNJf2n_ZvI

7. **Niluksi Koswanage**, **Eveline Danubrata**. Malaysia military source says missing jet veered to west. **Reuters** MARCH 11, 2014 https://www.reuters.com/article/malaysia-airlines/malaysia-military-source-says-missing-jet-veered-to-west-idINDEEA2900B20140311

8. Reuters (Chinese) . Malaysia Airlines incident: Malaysian military claims to have tracked missing Malaysia Airlines plane in Strait of Malacca. MARCH 11, 2014 https://www.reuters.com/article/malaysia-airlines-military-idCNL3S0M837I20140311

9. Malay military: Radar has tracked MH370 to the Strait of Malacca. China famous media._CCTV March 12, 2014 **04**: **15**[9]. http://tv.cctv.com/2014/03/12/VIDE1394568909534156.shtml

10._**Malay military: Radar has tracked MH370 to the Strait of Malacca. China famous media._CCTV March 12, 2014 21**: **21**[10]https://tv.cctv.com/2014/03/11/VIDE139454405943630 7.shtml

11. Wuyuanchun. Reuters: Malaysian military says radar monitors missing airliner flying over Strait of Malacca
World Wide Web. https://m.huanqiu.com/article/9CaKrnJExLL

12. Malay military: Radar detects missing airliner flying to Strait of Malacca. China Court International Website 2014-03-11 .

https://www.chinacourt.org/article/detail/2014/03/id/1228279.shtml

13. Malay military: Radar detects missing airliner flying to Strait of MalaccaChina Daily. 2014-03-11

https://world.chinadaily.com.cn/2014-03/11/content_17340023.htm

14. **Malaysia denies detecting missing plane in Strait of Malacca** . BBC News2014-03-12.

https://www.bbc.com/zhongwen/simp/world/2014/03/140312_malaysia_airlines

15. The Malaysian military denies that the passenger plane turned back to the Strait of Malacca. Mar 12, 2014
https://youtu.be/YeMy4IIIOhk

16._**Statement by TUDM Chief on Berita Harian report on Malaysia Airlines Flight MH370 March 12, 2014**

http://kementah.blogspot.com/2014/03/statement-by-tudm-chief-on-berita.html

17. Zhong Shan said: Malaysia Airline, Malaysia Government, what are you doing? Mar 14, 2014 **https://youtu.be/y-P7R9BEAvU**

18. Geoffrey Thomas. MH370 TRACKING MEETING "A GREAT SUCCESS". January 21, 2023.
https://www.airlineratings.com/news/mh370-tracking-meeting-a-great-success/

Lightning Source UK Ltd.
Milton Keynes UK
UKHW010700160223
417122UK00019B/1711